Contents

Meet the marsupials!

Marsupials are animals. There are many kinds of marsupials. Each marsupial belongs to a group. Some of the groups are shown on these pages.

koala

kangaroo

wombat

The marsupials on this page belong to the same group.

What Kind of Animal Is It?

Koalas and Other Marsupials

Bobbie Kalman & Robin Johnson

A Crabtree Crown Book

Crabtree Publishing

crabtreebooks.com

Koalas and Other Marsupials

Editor-in-chief
Bobbie Kalman

Writing team
Bobbie Kalman
Robin Johnson

Substantive editors
Amanda Bishop
Kelley MacAulay

Editors
Molly Aloian
Reagan Miller
Kathryn Smithyman

Design
Margaret Salter

Consultant
Patricia Loesche, Ph.D., Animal Behavior Program, Department of Psychology, University of Washington

Production manager
Candice Campbell

Images
Bonna Rouse: pages 7, 32 (lungs); ardea.com Mike Gilliam: page 25; Wikimedia Commons/dnathesit: page 23 (bottom left), 32 (planigale); Wikimedia Commons/Geoff Shaw: page 9 (top right); Wikimedia Commons/Museums Victoria: page 5, 32 (marsupial mole); all other images by Shutterstock.com

Crabtree Publishing

crabtreebooks.com 800-387-7650

In Canada: We acknowledge the financial support of the Government of Canada through the Canada Book Fund for our publishing activities.

Printed in the U.S.A./CP032026

Published in Canada
Crabtree Publishing
616 Welland Ave.
St. Catharines,
Ontario L2M 5V6

Published in the United States
Crabtree Publishing
347 Fifth Ave.
Suite 1402-145
New York, NY 10016

Hardcover: 978-1-0398-7319-3
Paperback: 978-1-0398-7377-3
Ebook (pdf): 978-1-0398-7426-8
Epub: 978-1-0398-7475-6

Library and Archives Canada Cataloguing in Publication
Available at Library and Archives Canada

Library of Congress Cataloging-in-Publication Data
Available at the Library of Congress

Bandicoots and bilbies belong to another marsupial group.

bandicoot

bilby

Marsupial moles form another marsupial group.

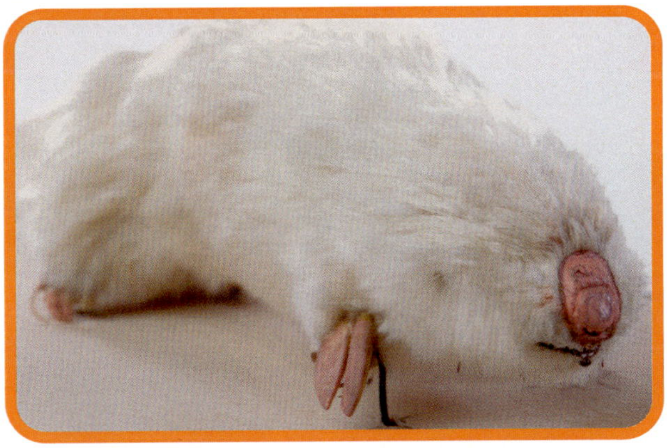

Opossums make up their own marsupial group.

Tasmanian devils and numbats belong to yet another marsupial group.

numbat

Tasmanian devil

A koala is a mammal. It is a warm-blooded animal.

Marsupials are mammals

Marsupials are **mammals**. Mammals are animals that are **warm-blooded**. The bodies of warm-blooded animals stay about the same temperature, even when the weather is hot or cold. Most marsupials live in places where the weather is hot.

A breath of fresh air

Mammals breathe air using **lungs**. Lungs are body parts that are inside mammals. Lungs take in air. They also let out air. A brushtail possum's lungs are shown below.

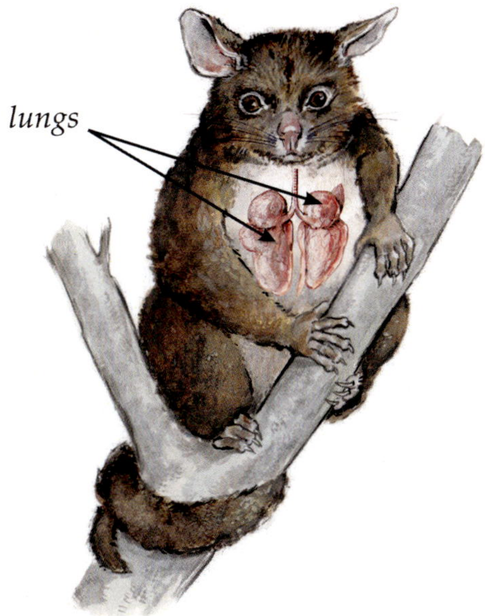

How are kangaroos and people the same? They are both mammals!

More about mammals

Mammals are animals that

- **nurse** when they are babies (See page 9.)
- have fur or hair on their bodies (See page 10.)
- have **backbones** (See page 11.)

A mother's pouch

Kangaroos have the largest pouches of any marsupial. This kangaroo baby is peeking out of its mother's pouch.

The word "marsupial" means "**pouch**." Pouches are pockets that most female marsupials have on the front of their bodies. Marsupial mothers feed and carry their babies in the pouches. Male marsupials do not have pouches.

The quokka baby, shown below, is warm and safe in its mother's pouch.

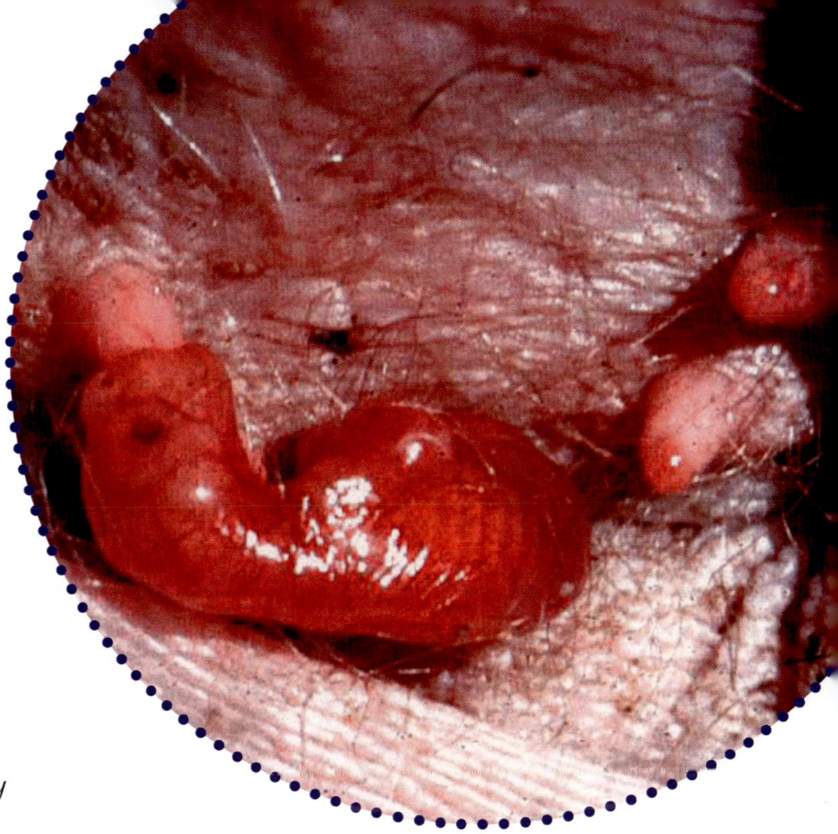

Marsupial babies

A marsupial baby is called a **joey**. As soon as a joey is born, it crawls into its mother's pouch. The joey grows in the pouch. It stays there for many weeks or months. Inside the pouch, the joey drinks milk from its mother's body. Drinking mother's milk is called nursing.

Did you know that most newborn joeys are the size of jellybeans? This tiny kangaroo joey is nursing inside its mother's pouch.

No pouches

A few marsupial mothers do not have pouches on their bodies. Their babies still nurse and grow, however. The marsupial mothers take care of their babies without using pouches. The numbat, shown left, is a marsupial that does not have a pouch.

Marsupial bodies

Marsupial bodies are different in some ways. They are also the same in some ways. These pages show a few of the ways in which marsupial bodies are the same.

Many marsupials have large ***snouts****. Snouts are noses. Marsupials use their snouts to find food to eat.*

Many marsupials have big ears. They can hear sounds from far away.

Like most mammals, marsupials have fur on their bodies. Fur keeps marsupials warm when the weather is cool.

Most marsupials have tails. A kangaroo's tail is long and strong. It helps the kangaroo balance while the animal is hopping.

Some marsupial mothers have pouches that open toward their tails. A koala's pouch opens toward its tail. Other marsupial mothers have pouches that open toward their heads.

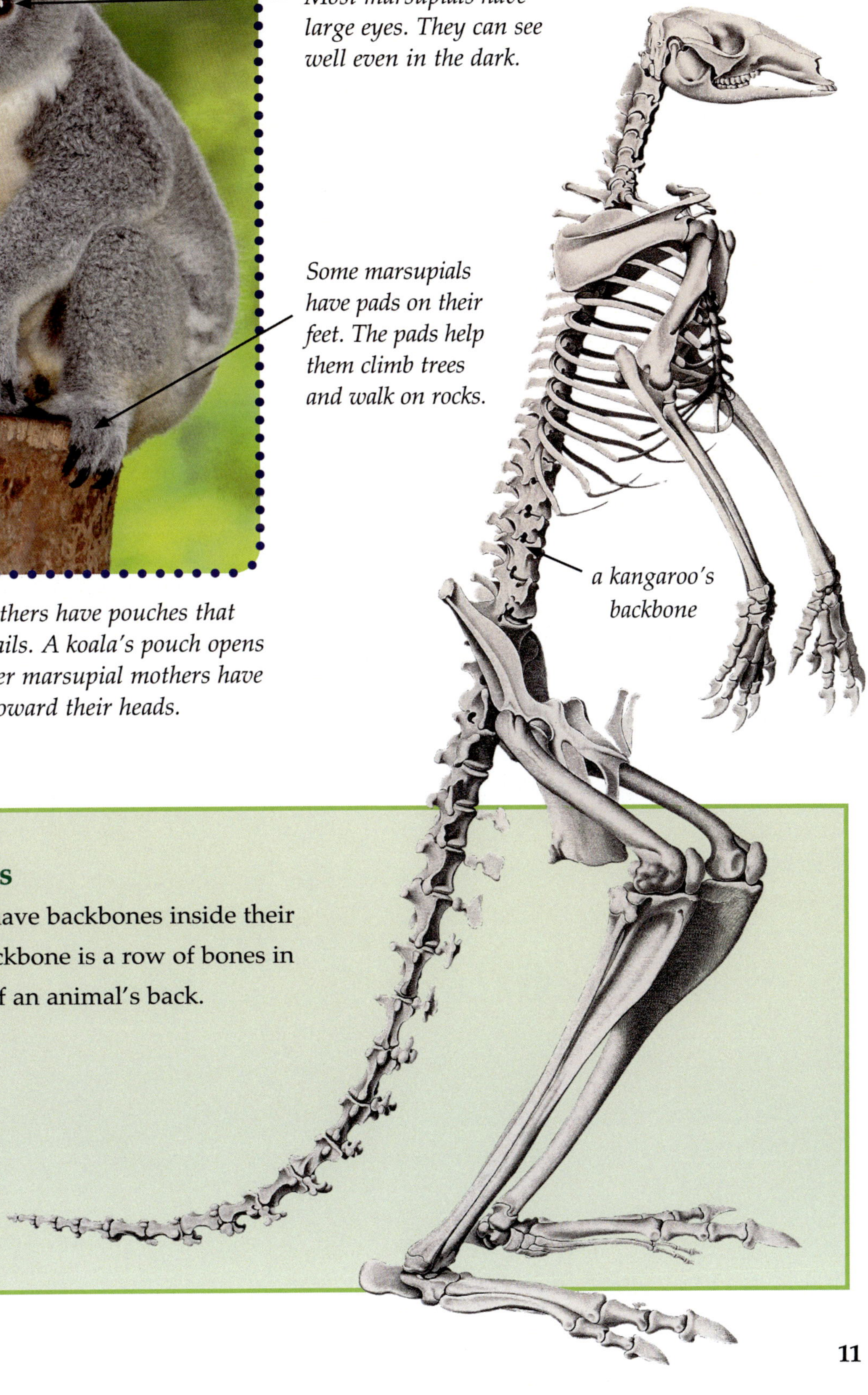

Backbones

Marsupials have backbones inside their bodies. A backbone is a row of bones in the middle of an animal's back.

Marsupials on the move

Different marsupials move in different ways. Most marsupials can swim. Some marsupials walk or run. Others hop. These pages show some of the ways that marsupials move.

Wombats walk or run on their short, thick legs. They can also swim.

Most kangaroos cannot walk. They must move their back legs together, so they hop. Kangaroos can hop quickly. Some large kangaroos can hop faster than horses can run!

Wild moves!

Tasmanian devils sometimes stomp their feet and jump quickly from side to side. They look like they are spinning around in circles! Tasmanian devils move this way and scream loudly to scare away other animals. It usually works!

*Gliders move from tree to tree by **gliding**. To glide means to sail through the air.*

Where do marsupials live?

Most marsupials live in Australia and on islands near Australia. The weather in Australia is usually hot. Most marsupials rest during the day to keep cool. At night, they look for food to eat. The kangaroo shown above is resting on the grass.

Marsupial habitats

Marsupials live in different **habitats**. Habitats are the natural places where animals live. Some marsupials live in forest habitats. Common opossums, shown right, live in forests. Other marsupial habitats are rocky hills, grassy fields, or sandy deserts.

Common opossums are the only marsupials that live in North America.

Living alone

Most marsupials live alone. Many have **home ranges** in their habitats. A home range is the area in which an animal lives. A marsupial that has a home range looks for food, eats, and sleeps in its home range.

This spotted cuscus lives in the trees in its home range. It will fight other cuscuses to keep them out of its home range.

What do marsupials eat?

Different marsupials eat different foods. Most marsupials are **herbivores**. Herbivores are animals that eat mainly plants. Marsupial herbivores eat grass, leaves, and roots.

This kangaroo eats grass and other plants. It is a herbivore.

Meat-eating marsupials

Some marsupials are **carnivores**. Carnivores are animals that eat other animals. Marsupial carnivores eat insects, birds, and reptiles. A few kinds of marsupials are **omnivores**. Omnivores are animals that eat both plants and animals.

Bilbies are marsupial omnivores. They eat insects and other small animals. They also eat seeds and fruit.

When Tasmanian devils find an animal to eat, they eat every part of the animal—even the bones!

Eat your water!

Did you know that most marsupial herbivores and omnivores do not need to drink water? They get the water they need from the plants they eat.

Koalas live in trees

Koalas are not bears! They are marsupials that live in **eucalyptus trees**. Eucalyptus trees are tall trees that grow in Australia. The leaves of eucalyptus trees are the only food that koalas eat. When koalas are not eating leaves, they are usually sleeping.

Koalas must eat many leaves each day in order to grow and stay healthy.

Sleepy koalas

Did you know that some koalas sleep up to eighteen hours each day? They sleep high in the branches of eucalyptus trees, as shown on the left. They are sleepy marsupials!

Koal-ity care

Koala mothers take good care of their babies. The mothers carry their babies with them wherever they go. A koala mother carries a young joey in her pouch. When the joey becomes too big for the pouch, the koala mother carries the joey on her back. A koala mother cares for her joey until the joey can live on its own.

When a koala joey is separated from its mother, the joey cries loudly until it finds its mother again.

Kangaroo mobs

Kangaroos often live with other kangaroos in groups. Groups of kangaroos are called **mobs**. Some mobs have only a few kangaroos. Other mobs have many kangaroos. There may be as many as a hundred kangaroos in a mob!

How many kangaroos are in this mob?

Tree kangaroos

Did you know that some kangaroos live in trees? They are called tree kangaroos. Tree kangaroos are the only kangaroos that can move one back leg at a time. Moving one leg at a time allows tree kangaroos to climb trees and to walk on tree branches.

Big family, big feet

Kangaroos belong to a large family of marsupials. The marsupials in this family all have big back feet. The family includes kangaroos, wallabies, wallaroos, pademelons, and quokkas. A rock wallaby is shown left.

Tasmanian devils

Tasmanian devils are the largest marsupial carnivores. They have strong bodies and sharp teeth. Tasmanian devils eat birds, reptiles, and other marsupials. In fact, Tasmanian devils will eat just about anything they can find!

Chew on this!
Did you know that Tasmanian devils have very strong jaws? Their jaws are as strong as the jaws of crocodiles and sharks!

Quolls and planigales

Quolls are marsupial carnivores. They look like cats, so people often call them marsupial cats. Quolls have sharp teeth and claws for hunting. They hunt birds, lizards, and even small kangaroos!

The spots on a quoll's fur blend in with its habitat. Blending in helps a quoll hide while it is hunting.

Planigales

Planigales are the smallest marsupials. Do not let their size fool you, though! Like quolls, these animals are fierce hunters. Some planigales even catch and eat animals that are bigger than they are!

This narrow-nosed planigale is looking for food. It eats insects and small lizards.

Wombats

Wombats live in underground homes called **burrows**. The burrows are made up of many long tunnels. Wombats sleep and hide from **predators** in their burrows. Predators are animals that hunt other animals for food.

Wombat mothers have pouches that open toward their tails. While the mothers dig burrows through the dirt, the joeys inside the pouches stay clean.

Wombats come out of their burrows only to look for food to eat.

Marsupial moles

Marsupial moles are tiny animals that spend most of their lives under ground. They live in deserts. They move by pushing their bodies through sand. When marsupial moles move, they look like they are swimming under ground!

Marsupial moles are blind because they do not need to see under ground.

Marsupial moles often come out of the sand to eat. They eat insects and other small animals. This marsupial mole is eating a lizard.

Numbats

Numbats are the only marsupials that are active during the day. They spend their days looking for food to eat. Numbats eat mainly termites and ants. They use their long, sticky tongues to lick up their **prey**. Prey are animals that predators eat.

Numbats have long, sharp claws. They use their claws to dig up food to eat.

Bandicoots

Bandicoots are omnivores. They use their sharp claws to dig up plants and small animals to eat. When they are not looking for food, bandicoots sleep in nests. Bandicoots use grass and other plants to make their nests.

This northern brown bandicoot is looking for food near its nest.

Opossums

Opossums have useful tails. They can hold and carry objects using their tails. Opossums also use their tails to climb trees. Some young opossums can even hang upside down by their tails!

This common opossum hangs around in North America.

Possibly possums

Did you know that there are also marsupials called possums? Possums and opossums are not the same. They belong to different marsupial groups and live in different places. A brushtail possum is shown above.

Gliders

Gliders are marsupials that can glide through the air. They have furry flaps of skin between their front and back legs. To take off, gliders jump from trees. They then stretch their arms and legs far apart. In this position, the wind carries them from one tree to another. As they glide from tree to tree, gliders seem to be flying through the air!

Gliders can travel long distances in the air. Some gliders can "fly" the length of a football field!

Move like a marsupial!

In this book you have seen that marsupials move in many ways. Now it is your turn to move like a marsupial!

Tasmanian devils sometimes look like they are spinning. Do you spin when you dance?

Kangaroos hop quickly. Hop like a kangaroo!

Marsupial moles use their claws to dig through sand. How do you dig in the sand?

Make sure an adult is with you when you are climbing or hanging upside down!

Hang upside down like a young opossum!

Words to know and Index

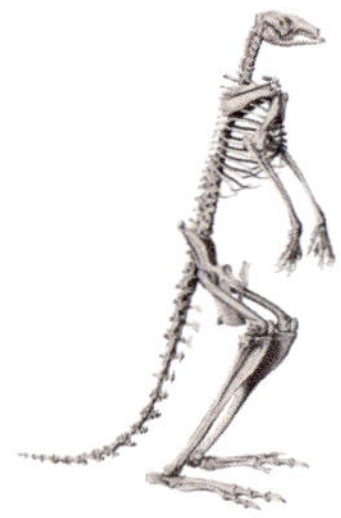

Other index words